"RIDING THE ROLLERCOASTER: NAVIGATING THE UPS AND DOWNS OF LIFE"

NAYANIKA NATH

Made with ♥ on the Notion Press Platform
www.notionpress.com

To my beloved father Utpal Kanti Nath and my mother Sunanda Nath.

This book would not have been possible without your love, support and encouragement. Thankyou for being my constant source of inspiration and motivation. Your belief in me has propelled me to pursue my dreams and share my voice with the world.

I dedicate this book to you also as a symbol of my gratitude and appreciation for all that you have done for me. May this work be a testament to the bond we share and the meaningful impact you have had on my life.

With love and admiration,

Nayanika Nath

Contents

Contents

Foreword

Dear reader,

It is with great pleasure that I present you this book. As a author, I have poured my heart and soul into these pages, and I sincerely hope that you find them engaging, thought provoking, and englightening. This book is cumilation of years of research, personal experience, and reflection. It delves into a range of topics, from the complexities of human relationships to the mysteries of universe. It seeks to challenge and inspire, to provoke and entertain, and to offer insights that will help you to navigate the twists and turns of life .

Asyou read through these pages, I encourage you to approach each chapter with an open mind and an eagerness to learn. Some of the ideas presented maybe familiar to you, while others maybe entirely new. Regardless of your prior knowledge, I hope that this book will deepen your understanding of the world around you and give you fresh prespectives on the issues that matters most.

I would like to take a moment to thanks those who have supported me throughout the writing of this book. To my family and close friends, who have encouraged me every step of the way, I am forever grateful. To my editor, who has worked tirelessly to polish these pages to perfection, I owe debt of gratitude.

Finally, I want to thank you, the reader, for choosing to embark on this journey with me. It is my sincere hope that this book will enrich your life in ways that you cannot yet imagine.

Sincerely, (Nayanika Nath)

Preface

Writing a book is no small feat. It requires dedication, discipline and passion for sharing ideas and stories with others. As the author of this book, I have poured my heart and souls into its pages, hoping to offer readers a glimpse into my world and the insights I have gained along the way.

This book is the culmination of my experiences, my thoughts and my aspirations. It is a labour of love that has taken me on a journey of self-discovery and growth. Through the pages of this book, I hope to inspire, inform and entertain reader, providing them with a new prespective on life and the world around us.

Whether you are reading this book for pleasure or for learning, I invite you to join me on this journey. Let us explore depth of our mind, the beauty of our surroundings, and the power of our humanity together. Let us open our heart and minds to new possibilities and discover the wonders of the world around us.

Prologue

Life is an unpredictable journey full of ups and downs. At times, we experience moments of immense joy and happiness, where everything seems to fall into place. We cherish these moments and hold onto them tightly, hoping they will last forever. However, just as quickly as they came, they fade away, leaving us feeling lost and uncertain. On the other hand, life can also throw us into a whirlwind of chaos and despair. We may face difficult challenges that seem insurmountable, leaving us feeling overwhelmed and hopeless. In these moments, we may question our purpose and wonder if we will ever find our way back to happiness.

However, it is important to remember that both the ups and downs of life are necessary for growth and self-discovery. It is through our struggles that we learn resilience, perseverance, and strength. And it is through our moments of joy that we learn to appreciate and cherish the beauty of life.

Ultimately, life is a journey full of twists and turns, and it is up to us to navigate these challenges with grace and courage. By embracing both the highs and lows, we can live a life that is rich, meaningful, and full of purpose.

CHAPTER ONE

The Power of Perspective: Seeing Life's Ups and Downs in a New Light

Life is full of ups and downs. Sometimes, things go exactly as we plan and we feel like we are on top of the world. Other times, unexpected obstacles arise and we feel like everything is falling apart. How we choose to perceive these ups and downs can greatly impact our mental and emotional well-being.

Perspective is a powerful tool that can help us see the world in a different light. It refers to the way we view things and can greatly influence our thoughts, feelings, and actions. When we change our perspective, we can change our entire outlook on life.

One way to shift our perspective is to focus on the positive aspects of a situation. Even when things don't go according to plan, there is always something to be grateful for. Maybe we learned something new, had a valuable experience, or gained a new perspective. By focusing on the positive, we can reframe the situation and see it in a new light.

For example, imagine you lose your job. At first, it may seem like a devastating blow. However, by shifting your perspective, you may realize that this is an opportunity to explore new career paths, spend more time with your family, or even take a well-deserved break. By focusing on the positive aspects of the situation, you can turn a negative experience into a positive one.

Another way to shift our perspective is to practice empathy. This involves putting ourselves in someone else's shoes and trying to see things from their perspective. By doing so, we can gain a better understanding of their actions and emotions.

For example, imagine you are in a heated argument with a friend. Instead of getting defensive and trying to prove your point, try to understand their perspective. What experiences, emotions, or beliefs may be influencing their opinion? By practicing empathy, you can diffuse the situation and find a resolution that works for both of you.

A third way to shift our perspective is to embrace change. Change can be scary and uncomfortable, but it is also an opportunity for growth and self-discovery. When we embrace change, we open ourselves up to new experiences and possibilities.

For example, imagine you are moving to a new city. Instead of focusing on the things you will miss about your current home, embrace the opportunity to explore a new place, meet new people, and try new things. By embracing change, you can turn a potentially stressful situation into an exciting adventure.Finally, it is important to remember that our perspective is not set in stone. It can change and evolve over time as we gain new experiences and knowledge.

What once seemed impossible may now be within reach. What once seemed insurmountable may now seem manageable.For example, imagine you have a fear of public speaking. At first, the thought of giving a speech may seem daunting and impossible. However, as you gain more experience and practice, you may realize that public speaking is not as scary as you once thought. By changing your perspective, you can overcome your fear and accomplish things you never thought possible.In conclusion, the power of perspective is a valuable tool that can help us navigate life's ups and downs. By focusing on the positive, practicing empathy, embracing change, and remaining open to new experiences, we can shift our perspective and see the world in a new light. As we do so, we can become more resilient, adaptable, and open-minded individuals.

CHAPTER TWO

From Darkness to Light: Overcoming Life's Darkest Moments

From darkness to light, the journey of overcoming life's darkest moments is never an easy one. It takes strength, courage, and resilience to navigate through the challenges that life throws at us. But with determination and the right mindset, it is possible to find hope and light in even the darkest of times.

The journey begins with acknowledging and accepting the darkness. It can be difficult to face the pain, hurt, and suffering that comes with difficult times, but it is important to acknowledge them and accept them as a part of the journey. Only by facing our fears and vulnerabilities can we begin to overcome them.

As we begin to navigate through the darkness, it is important to find a support system. Surrounding ourselves with people who love and care for us can provide us with the strength and encouragement we need to keep moving forward. They can be our rock, our support, and our source of light when we feel lost and alone.

Another key aspect of overcoming life's darkest moments is finding meaning and purpose. When we are faced with adversity, it can be easy to lose sight of our purpose and goals. But by finding meaning in our struggles, we can turn our pain into purpose and use our experiences to help others.

Forgiveness is another important aspect of the journey from darkness to light. Holding onto anger, resentment, and bitterness can keep us trapped in the darkness. It is important to forgive ourselves and others, and to let go of the past so that we can move forward and find peace.

Faith and spirituality can also provide comfort and guidance during difficult times. Whether through prayer, meditation, or other spiritual practices, connecting with a higher power can help us find hope and strength in even the darkest of times.

As we begin to navigate through the darkness, it is important to take care of ourselves both physically and mentally. Eating well, getting enough sleep, and engaging in regular exercise can help us feel stronger and more resilient. Seeking professional help from a therapist or counselor can also be a valuable tool in overcoming life's darkest moments.

Self-reflection and introspection are also important aspects of the journey from darkness to light. Taking time to reflect on our experiences and emotions can help us gain clarity and understanding, and can help us identify areas for growth and improvement.

As we continue to move forward, it is important to maintain a positive mindset. Focusing on the positive aspects of our lives, practicing gratitude, and surrounding ourselves with positivity can help us stay hopeful and optimistic during difficult times.

Finally, it is important to celebrate our progress and accomplishments along the way. Each step forward, no matter how small, is a victory to be celebrated. By acknowledging our progress, we can stay motivated and inspired to continue moving towards the light.

In conclusion, the journey from darkness to light is a challenging one, but it is possible to overcome life's darkest moments with determination, strength, and resilience. By accepting the darkness, finding support, forgiveness, meaning and purpose, faith and spirituality, self-care, self-reflection, positivity, and celebrating our progress, we can navigate through difficult times and find hope and light in even the darkest of moments.

CHAPTER THREE

When Life Throws You Curveballs: Coping with Unexpected Challenges

Life can be unpredictable, and when unexpected challenges arise, it can be difficult to cope. Whether it's a sudden illness, job loss, or a relationship ending, curveballs can throw us off balance and leave us feeling overwhelmed and unsure of how to move forward.

The first step in coping with unexpected challenges is to allow yourself to feel your emotions. It's normal to feel a range of emotions such as anger, sadness, and frustration. Acknowledging and accepting these emotions can help you process what you're going through and begin to work through them.

It's important to give yourself time and space to adjust to the new reality. You don't have to have all the answers right away. Take a step back, breathe, and give yourself permission to take things one day at a time.

One helpful way to cope with unexpected challenges is to focus on what you can control. While there may be things out of your control, there are still actions you can take to improve your situation. Focus on what you can do, such as making a plan, seeking support, or taking steps to improve your physical and mental health.

It's also important to seek support during difficult times. Talk to friends or family members you trust, or seek out a support group or therapist. Talking about what you're going through and receiving support can help you feel less alone and more empowered to move forward.

Practicing self-care is another important aspect of coping with unexpected challenges. Take time to engage in activities that make you feel good, such as exercise, reading, or spending time in nature. Taking care of your physical and mental health can help you feel more resilient and better able to cope with challenges.

Another helpful coping strategy is to reframe the situation. Instead of focusing on the negative aspects of the challenge, try to find any positive aspects or opportunities for growth. For example, a job loss can be an opportunity to explore a new career path or take a break to focus on personal growth.

It's also important to remember that setbacks are a natural part of life. No one has a perfect life, and everyone experiences challenges at some point. Instead of feeling defeated, try to see the challenge as a learning experience that can help you grow and become stronger.

One helpful way to cope with unexpected challenges is to practice mindfulness. Mindfulness involves being present in the moment and accepting your thoughts and feelings without judgment. Practicing mindfulness can help you feel more grounded and less overwhelmed by the situation.

It's also important to set realistic expectations for yourself. Don't put pressure on yourself to have everything figured out right away. Be patient and kind to yourself, and remember that progress takes time.

Finally, try to maintain a positive outlook. While it may be difficult to see the light at the end of the tunnel during challenging times, focusing on the positive aspects of your life can help you feel more hopeful and optimistic about the future.

In conclusion, unexpected challenges can be difficult to cope with, but there are strategies you can use to help you navigate through them. By allowing yourself to feel your emotions, focusing on what you can control, seeking support, practicing self-care, reframing the situation, accepting setbacks, practicing mindfulness, setting realistic expectations, and maintaining a positive outlook, you can build resilience and find a way to move forward when life throws you curveballs.

CHAPTER FOUR

Riding the Wave: How to Survive Life's Highs and Lows

Surviving Life's Highs.

Life is a journey full of ups and downs. We all experience moments of joy and moments of despair, moments of success and moments of failure. However, it's not just about experiencing those moments, but also about how we deal with them. Riding the wave is a skill that can help us navigate through life's highs and lows.

The first step in riding the wave is to accept that life is unpredictable. There will be moments when everything is going great, and there will be moments when everything seems to be falling apart. We can't control everything that happens to us, but we can control how we react to it. Accepting that life is unpredictable can help us develop resilience and strength to face challenges head-on.

Another important aspect of riding the wave is learning to stay present. It's easy to get caught up in past regrets or future anxieties, but doing so can lead to unnecessary stress and worry. By staying present, we can focus on the task at hand and avoid getting overwhelmed.

It's also important to have a support system in place. Surrounding ourselves with people who are positive, supportive, and empathetic can help us navigate through life's highs and lows. We all need someone to lean on when times get tough, and having a support system can make all the difference.

Finally, it's important to take care of ourselves. This means getting enough sleep, eating a healthy diet, and exercising regularly. When we take care of ourselves, we are better equipped to handle life's challenges.

In conclusion, riding the wave is about accepting the unpredictability of life, staying present, having a support system, and taking care of ourselves. By developing these skills, we can survive life's highs and lows and emerge stronger and more resilient than ever before.

CHAPTER FIVE

Finding the Silver Lining: Looking for the Positive in Negative Situations

Finding the silver lining is all about looking for the positive in negative situations. While it may seem challenging to find something positive in a difficult situation, it can be a powerful tool for improving your mood and mindset.

One way to find the silver lining is to focus on what you've learned or gained from the experience. Even if the situation was unpleasant, you may have learned a valuable lesson or gained a new perspective that can help you in the future.

Another way to find the silver lining is to focus on the present moment. Instead of dwelling on the negative aspects of the situation, try to appreciate the good things in your life right now. Practicing gratitude can help shift your mindset and make it easier to find the positive in negative situations.

It's also helpful to reframe the situation and look at it from a different perspective. Instead of seeing it as a setback, try to see it as an opportunity for growth or a chance to try something new.By finding the silver lining, you can shift your focus from the negative aspects of a situation to the positive. This can help improve your mood and mindset, and make it easier to navigate through challenging times.

CHAPTER SIX

Navigating Transitions: Coping with Life Changes, Big and Small

Life is full of transitions, both big and small. Some transitions are planned, such as going to college or getting married, while others are unexpected, like losing a job or experiencing a major illness. Navigating these transitions can be challenging, but there are strategies that can help us cope.

The first step in coping with transitions is to acknowledge and accept that change is a natural part of life. It's important to recognize that it's normal to feel anxious or overwhelmed during times of transition. Once we accept this, we can begin to focus on strategies that can help us cope.

One important strategy is to practice self-care. Taking care of our physical, emotional, and mental health is crucial during times of transition. This means getting enough sleep, eating a healthy diet, exercising, and taking time to relax and recharge.

It's also important to seek support from friends, family, or a professional therapist. Talking about our feelings with someone we trust can help us process our emotions and gain perspective on our situation.

Another strategy is to focus on the present moment. By staying present, we can avoid getting caught up in worries about the future or regrets about the past. Mindfulness practices, such as meditation or yoga, can be helpful in staying present and reducing stress.

In conclusion, navigating transitions can be challenging, but by acknowledging and accepting change, practicing self-care, seeking support, and staying present, we can cope with life's changes and come out stronger on the other side.

CHAPTER SEVEN

Growing Through Pain: How Tough Times Can Make You Stronger

Pain and difficult times are inevitable in life, but they can also be opportunities for growth and strength. When we experience pain, we are often forced to confront our weaknesses and vulnerabilities, which can ultimately lead to personal growth and a deeper understanding of ourselves.

One way to grow through pain is to practice resilience. Resilience is the ability to bounce back from adversity, and it can be cultivated through a variety of practices, such as meditation, exercise, and seeking support from others. By developing resilience, we can learn to handle difficult situations with grace and determination.

Another way to grow through pain is to practice self-reflection. When we experience pain, it's important to take the time to reflect on what we've learned from the experience. This can help us gain insight into ourselves and our values, and ultimately lead to personal growth and transformation.

It's also important to remember that pain can be a catalyst for positive change. Sometimes it takes a painful experience to push us out of our comfort zones and into new opportunities. By embracing the challenge and using it as an opportunity for growth, we can become stronger and more resilient individuals.

In conclusion, while pain and difficult times are never easy, they can also be opportunities for growth and strength. By practicing resilience, self-reflection, and embracing the challenge, we can learn to grow through pain and emerge stronger on the other side.

CHAPTER EIGHT

Learning to Let Go: Moving On from Life's Disappointments

Learning to let go is an important life skill that can help us move on from disappointments and setbacks. Whether it's a failed relationship, a missed opportunity, or an unfulfilled dream, holding onto the past can prevent us from enjoying the present and pursuing new opportunities.

One way to let go is to acknowledge our feelings and accept that it's okay to feel sad, angry, or disappointed. We can talk to friends or family, write in a journal, or seek professional help if needed. It's important to give ourselves time to process our emotions and not try to suppress them.

Another helpful approach is to focus on the present and the future. This can involve setting new goals, trying new activities, or making positive changes in our lives. By taking action and focusing on what we can control, we can shift our attention away from the past and towards a brighter future.

Finally, forgiveness can be a powerful tool for letting go. This doesn't mean forgetting what happened or excusing bad behavior, but rather letting go of resentment and anger towards ourselves or others. Forgiveness can help us find peace and move forward with a lighter heart.

Learning to let go is not always easy, but it's a skill that can be learned and practiced over time. By acknowledging our emotions, focusing on the present and the future, and practicing forgiveness, we can move on from life's disappointments and create a happier, more fulfilling life.

CHAPTER NINE

The Art of Resilience: Bouncing Back from Life's Setbacks

Resilience is the ability to bounce back from life's setbacks, whether it's a major illness, a job loss, or a relationship breakdown. While it's a natural human trait, it's also something that can be cultivated and strengthened over time.

One key to resilience is having a strong support network. This can include family, friends, and professional therapists who can offer guidance and support during difficult times. It's also important to develop strong coping mechanisms, such as exercise, meditation, and hobbies, that can help manage stress and boost mental health.

Another important factor is having a positive outlook. While it can be difficult to maintain positivity during challenging times, focusing on the good things in life can help build resilience and prevent negative thoughts from taking over. This can involve keeping a gratitude journal, practicing mindfulness, or engaging in positive self-talk.

Resilience also involves adaptability and flexibility. When faced with unexpected challenges, being able to adapt and find new solutions can help us bounce back stronger than ever. This can involve seeking out new opportunities, learning new skills, or finding creative ways to navigate challenges.In conclusion, resilience is an essential skill for navigating life's setbacks. By developing a strong support network, cultivating coping mechanisms, maintaining a positive outlook, and embracing adaptability, we can bounce back from setbacks and emerge stronger and more resilient than ever before.

CHAPTER TEN

Weathering the Storm: Strategies for Surviving Life's Toughest Moments

Life is full of unpredictable and challenging moments, and we often find ourselves facing tough situations that leave us feeling overwhelmed and helpless. Whether it's a job loss, a health crisis, or a relationship breakdown, weathering life's storms can be incredibly difficult. However, there are strategies we can use to help us survive these tough moments.The fourth strategy is to practice resilience. Resilience is the ability to bounce back from adversity, and it's a skill that can be cultivated over time. This can involve developing coping mechanisms, such as meditation or mindfulness, seeking out new opportunities, or focusing on the positive aspects of our lives.

The first strategy is to acknowledge and accept our emotions. It's natural to feel a range of emotions during tough times, including sadness, anger, and frustration.

Instead of pushing these emotions aside or pretending they don't exist, it's important to acknowledge them and allow ourselves to feel them fully. This can be challenging, but it's an essential step in processing our emotions and moving forward.

The second strategy is to build a support network. Having a strong support system can make a huge difference during tough times. This can include family, friends, colleagues, or even a professional therapist. Talking to someone who understands and empathizes with our situation can help us feel less alone and more supported.

The third strategy is to take care of ourselves. During tough times, it's easy to neglect our own needs and focus solely on the challenges we're facing. However, taking care of ourselves is essential for our mental and physical health. This can include getting enough sleep, eating well, and engaging in activities we enjoy, such as exercise or hobbies.

The fourth strategy is to practice resilience. Resilience is the ability to bounce back from adversity, and it's a skill that can be cultivated over time. This can involve developing coping mechanisms, such as meditation or mindfulness, seeking out new opportunities, or focusing on the positive aspects of our lives.

The fifth strategy is to find meaning in the experience. While it can be difficult to find meaning in tough situations, doing so can help us make sense of what's happened and move forward with greater clarity and purpose. This can involve reflecting on what we've learned from the experience, or finding ways to use our experience to help others.

Ultimately, weathering life's storms requires a combination of emotional, social, and practical strategies. By acknowledging our emotions, building a support network, taking care of ourselves, practicing resilience, and finding meaning in the experience, we can survive life's toughest moments and emerge stronger and more resilient on the other side.

It's also important to remember that tough times are temporary. While it may feel like the storm will never end, it will eventually pass, and we will come out on the other side. By holding onto hope and staying positive, we can weather the storm and emerge with a greater sense of strength and resilience.

In conclusion, weathering life's storms can be incredibly challenging, but there are strategies we can use to help us survive these tough moments. By acknowledging our emotions, building a support network, taking care of ourselves, practicing resilience, and finding meaning in the experience, we can navigate even the toughest of storms with greater strength and resilience

CHAPTER ELEVEN

Finding Joy in the Everyday: Celebrating Life's Small Victories

Life is a journey, and along the way, we experience ups and downs. There are moments of joy and moments of sorrow. We often celebrate the big victories, but we tend to overlook the small ones. However, finding joy in the everyday and celebrating life's small victories can have a significant impact on our well-being and overall happiness.

What are small victories, and why are they important? Small victories are the little things that happen throughout the day that make us feel good. They can be as simple as finishing a task at work, finding a parking spot close to the entrance, or having a pleasant conversation with a stranger. These small victories can seem insignificant, but they add up and contribute to our overall sense of happiness.

Celebrating small victories is essential because it helps us shift our focus from what's wrong to what's right. It's easy to get bogged down by the negative aspects of life, but celebrating small victories helps us see the positive. By focusing on the good things that happen throughout the day, we can improve our mood and outlook on life.

So, how can we find joy in the everyday and celebrate life's small victories? Here are some tips:

Practice gratitude: Gratitude is the practice of being thankful for what we have. When we focus on what we're grateful for, we can see the good in our lives. Take a few minutes each day to reflect on what you're grateful for. It can be anything from having a roof over your head to having a supportive family. Write down your thoughts in a gratitude journal, and refer back to it when you need a reminder of the good things in your life.

Set achievable goals: Setting goals is an excellent way to motivate yourself and feel a sense of accomplishment. However, it's essential to set achievable goals. When we set unrealistic goals, we're setting ourselves up for disappointment. Start small and work your way up. Celebrate the small victories along the way, and you'll feel a sense of progress and achievement.

Be present: It's easy to get caught up in the past or worry about the future. However, when we're always looking back or forward, we're missing out on the present moment. Take a few minutes each day to be present. Focus on your breath, notice your surroundings, and be grateful for the moment.

Celebrate progress, not just perfection: We often focus on achieving perfection, but the truth is, it's impossible to be perfect. Instead, focus on progress. Celebrate the small steps you take towards your goals. If you're trying to eat healthier, celebrate the day you chose a salad instead of a burger. If you're trying to save money, celebrate the day you didn't buy that expensive item you didn't really need.

Connect with others: Connection is essential for our well-being. When we connect with others, we feel a sense of belonging and purpose. Take time to connect with the people around you. Have a conversation with a coworker, call a friend, or spend time with your family. These small moments of connection can be a source of joy in our everyday lives.

Do something you enjoy: It's essential to take time for yourself and do something you enjoy. Whether it's reading a book, taking a walk, or watching your favorite TV show, make time for activities that bring you joy.

In conclusion, finding joy in the everyday and celebrating life's small victories is essential for our well-being and happiness. By focusing on the good things in our lives, we can improve our mood, outlook, and overall sense of happiness. Take time each day to practice gratitude, set achievable goals, be present, celebrate progress, connect with others, and do something you enjoy. These small things give you a eternal joy.

CHAPTER TWELVE

Taking Risks: Embracing the Ups and Downs of Adventure

Life is an adventure, and adventures often involve taking risks. Whether it's trying a new activity, starting a new career, or traveling to a foreign country, taking risks can be both exciting and daunting. While some risks may result in failure or disappointment, others can lead to incredible experiences and personal growth. In this article, we'll explore the ups and downs of adventure and how to embrace taking risks in our lives.

Why Taking Risks is Important

Taking risks can be scary, but it's essential for personal growth and development. When we take risks, we step outside of our comfort zone and push ourselves to grow and learn. It can also lead to new experiences and opportunities that we may not have had otherwise.

Taking risks can also help us overcome fear and build resilience. When we face our fears and take risks, we learn that we're capable of handling challenging situations. This can lead to increased confidence and a sense of empowerment.

However, it's essential to note that not all risks are created equal. It's important to weigh the potential benefits and consequences of a risk before taking it. It's also essential to take calculated risks and not put ourselves or others in harm's way.

The Ups of Adventure

The ups of adventure are the positive experiences and benefits that come with taking risks. Here are some of the benefits of embracing adventure and taking risks:

Increased Confidence: Taking risks can lead to increased confidence and self-esteem. When we accomplish something challenging, we feel proud of ourselves and our abilities. This can lead to increased self-confidence in other areas of our lives.

Personal Growth: Taking risks can lead to personal growth and development. When we face challenges and overcome them, we learn new skills and develop new strengths. This can lead to increased self-awareness and personal growth.

New Experiences: Taking risks can lead to new experiences and opportunities that we may not have had otherwise. Whether it's traveling to a new country, trying a new activity, or starting a new career, taking risks can lead to incredible experiences that enrich our lives.

Overcoming Fear: Taking risks can help us overcome fear and build resilience. When we face our fears and take risks, we learn that we're capable of handling challenging situations. This can lead to increased confidence and a sense of empowerment.

The Downs of Adventure

The downs of adventure are the potential negative consequences and challenges that come with taking risks.

Here are some of the challenges of embracing adventure and taking risks:

Failure: Taking risks can lead to failure and disappointment. When we take risks, there's always a chance that things won't work out as we planned. This can lead to feelings of frustration and disappointment.

Uncertainty: Taking risks can be uncertain and unpredictable. We don't always know how things will turn out.

Taking risks can be scary and uncomfortable, but it can also lead to some of the most rewarding experiences in life. Embracing the ups and downs of adventure means being open to new opportunities, even if they come with a certain level of uncertainty or risk.

One of the biggest benefits of taking risks is the potential for personal growth and development. When we step outside of our comfort zones and try new things, we learn about ourselves and what we're capable of. We develop resilience and become better equipped to handle challenges in the future.

Another benefit of taking risks is the potential for excitement and fulfillment. When we take a chance on something, we're often rewarded with a sense of adventure and excitement. We may also discover new passions and interests that we never knew we had.

Of course, taking risks also comes with the potential for failure or disappointment. It's important to acknowledge these possibilities and prepare ourselves for the potential downsides. However, even when things don't go as planned, we can still learn and grow from the experience.

Ultimately, taking risks is about living life to the fullest and embracing all of its ups and downs. It's about challenging ourselves and pushing beyond our limits, even if it means taking a leap of faith. By embracing the adventure of life, we can find new opportunities for personal growth, fulfillment, and excitement.

Last but not the least,
Taking risks can be both beneficial and detrimental, depending on how they are approached. On the one hand, taking risks can lead to new opportunities, growth, and success. It can also be a source of excitement and adventure. By stepping out of our comfort zones and taking calculated risks, we can gain valuable experiences and learn new skills.

On the other hand, taking risks can also lead to negative consequences, such as failure, disappointment, and loss. If risks are taken without careful consideration, they can lead to negative outcomes that can have a lasting impact on our lives. Additionally, taking risks can cause stress and anxiety, which can have a detrimental effect on our mental health and well-being.

Therefore, it's essential to weigh the pros and cons before taking risks. It's crucial to consider the potential benefits, as well as the potential consequences. Calculated risks, where potential outcomes have been evaluated and considered, are often the most successful. It's also important to remember that not all risks are worth taking, and it's okay to say no if it doesn't align with our values or goals.

In conclusion, taking risks can be both beneficial and detrimental. It's important to consider the potential benefits and consequences before taking risks and to take calculated risks that align with our values and goals. By embracing the ups and downs of adventure, we can gain valuable experiences, grow, and ultimately live a more fulfilling life.

CHAPTER THIRTEEN

Building Resilient Communities: Finding Strength in Connection and Support

Building resilient communities involves creating a network of people who can support each other in times of need. Resilience is the ability to overcome adversity and challenges, and a resilient community is one that can come together to support its members during times of stress, disaster, or other difficult situations.

The foundation of a resilient community is connection. People who are connected to each other are more likely to help each other in times of need. This can mean anything from having a friendly neighbor to call on for help to participating in a community organization that helps those in need. When people are connected, they are more likely to share resources and information, which can help everyone in the community.

Support is also key to building a resilient community. When people feel supported, they are more likely to bounce back from difficult situations. Support can come in many forms, such as emotional support from friends and family, financial support from a community organization, or practical support from neighbors and volunteers.

One way to build resilience in a community is to encourage volunteerism. Volunteering is a great way to connect with others and to contribute to the community. When people volunteer, they not only help others, but they also feel good about themselves and their contributions. This can lead to a sense of purpose and belonging, which can be very important during times of stress.

Another way to build resilience in a community is to create spaces for people to come together. This can be anything from a community center to a park. When people have places to gather and connect, they are more likely to build relationships and support each other. These spaces can also be used for community events and activities, which can help to strengthen the sense of community.

Communication is also important in building resilience. When people are informed about what is happening in their community, they are better prepared to respond to challenges. This can mean anything from sharing information about weather events to letting people know about community resources that are available. When people are informed, they can make better decisions and take action to protect themselves and their community.

Finally, it's important to recognize that building resilience is an ongoing process. Communities must be prepared to adapt and change as new challenges arise. This means being open to new ideas and strategies, and being willing to learn from other communities that have faced similar challenges. Building resilience takes time and effort, but it's worth it to create a community that is strong and supportive.

In conclusion, building resilient communities involves creating connections between people and providing support when it's needed. By encouraging volunteerism, creating spaces for people to come together, communicating effectively, and being willing to adapt and change, communities can become more resilient and better prepared to face whatever challenges come their way.

CHAPTER FOURTEEN

Embracing the Ups and Downs of Adventure: Celebrating Life's Ups and Downs and Everything In Between

Celebrating life's ups and downs.
Life is an adventure. It's full of ups and downs, twists and turns, and unexpected surprises. Embracing the ups and downs of adventure means learning to celebrate every moment, whether good or bad. It means understanding that life is not always perfect, but that every experience can teach us something valuable.

The ups of life's adventure are easy to celebrate. These are the moments when everything seems to be going our way. We get that promotion at work, we meet the love of our life, we win the big game. These moments fill us with happiness and give us a sense of accomplishment. We should celebrate these moments with gratitude and humility, recognizing that not everyone is as fortunate as we are.

But what about the downs of life's adventure? These are the moments when things don't go as planned. We lose our job, we experience a break-up, we get a bad diagnosis. These moments can be difficult and painful, but they can also be opportunities for growth and learning. Instead of dwelling on the negative, we should embrace these moments as part of our adventure and look for the lessons they can teach us.

One of the biggest lessons we can learn from the downs of life's adventure is resilience. When things get tough, we have a choice to make. We can give up, or we can keep pushing forward. Resilience means choosing to keep going, even when the road ahead seems difficult. It means learning from our mistakes and using them as stepping stones to future success.

Another important lesson we can learn from the downs of life's adventure is empathy. When we experience difficult times, we become more aware of the struggles that others are facing. We become more compassionate and understanding, and we are better able to connect with those around us. This empathy can help us build stronger relationships and make a positive impact on the world around us.

Embracing the ups and downs of adventure also means embracing the in-between moments. These are the times when life seems to be moving along at a steady pace, without any major highs or lows. These moments may not be as exciting as the ups or as challenging as the downs, but they are just as important. They give us time to reflect on where we've been and where we're going. They allow us to appreciate the simple joys of life and the people we share it with.

Celebrating life's ups and downs and everything in between requires a certain mindset. It requires us to let go of the idea that life should be perfect all the time. It requires us to accept that there will be difficult moments, but that these moments do not define us. It requires us to be grateful for the good times, but to also find meaning in the challenging times.

In conclusion, life is an adventure full of ups and downs. Embracing this adventure means celebrating every moment, whether good or bad. It means learning from our mistakes and using them as opportunities for growth. It means building resilience and empathy, and appreciating the in-between moments. By embracing the ups and downs of adventure, we can live a more fulfilling and meaningful life.

CHAPTER FIFTEEN

The Importance of Self-Care: Managing Life's Stressors

Self-care is essential for managing life's stressors. It involves taking steps to prioritize your own physical, mental, and emotional well-being, and can help you feel more resilient and better equipped to handle the challenges that come your way. Whether you are dealing with work-related stress, family responsibilities, or other external pressures, self-care can help you maintain a sense of balance and perspective, and avoid burning out or becoming overwhelmed.

One key aspect of self-care is maintaining healthy habits related to sleep, exercise, and nutrition. Getting enough sleep is crucial for both physical and mental health, and can help improve your mood, concentration, and overall well-being. Similarly, regular exercise can help reduce stress, boost mood, and improve physical health. Eating a healthy, balanced diet that includes plenty of fruits, vegetables, lean protein, and whole grains can provide the fuel your body needs to function at its best, and can help you feel more energized and alert.

Another important aspect of self-care is setting boundaries and managing your time effectively. This might involve learning to say no to commitments that are not essential, delegating tasks to others when possible, and prioritizing your own needs and goals. By taking control of your time and setting clear boundaries, you can reduce feelings of overwhelm and ensure that you have enough time and energy to devote to the things that matter most to you.

In addition to these physical and practical aspects of self-care, it is also important to attend to your emotional and mental well-being. This might involve practicing mindfulness, meditation, or other relaxation techniques, seeking support from friends or a mental health professional, and engaging in activities that bring you joy and fulfillment. By taking time to nurture your emotional well-being, you can cultivate a greater sense of resilience, cope more effectively with stress, and enjoy a more balanced and fulfilling life.

One challenge of practicing self-care is that it can feel self-indulgent or selfish, particularly for those who are used to putting others' needs before their own. However, it is important to remember that taking care of yourself is not a luxury or a selfish act, but rather a necessary component of maintaining your own health and well-being. When you prioritize your own self-care, you are better able to show up for the people and responsibilities in your life with greater energy, focus, and presence.In today's fast-paced world, it can be easy to neglect self-care in favor of meeting external demands and expectations. However, by taking steps to prioritize your own well-being, you can manage life's stressors more effectively, maintain a sense of balance and perspective, and enjoy a more fulfilling and rewarding life. Whether you choose to practice self-care through healthy habits, boundary-setting, emotional self-care, or other strategies, the key is to make it a priority and to approach it with a sense of intention and purpose. By doing so, you can cultivate greater resilience and well-being, and thrive in the face of life's challenges.

CHAPTER SIXTEEN

The Gift of Feedback: Using Criticism as a Stepping Stone to Success

Feedback is an essential part of personal and professional growth. It allows us to gain insights into our strengths and weaknesses, and identify areas where we can improve. However, feedback is often associated with criticism, which can be difficult to receive. Many people view criticism as a negative experience that can harm their self-esteem and motivation. But, feedback can be used as a stepping stone to success if we learn to receive and use it effectively.

The first step in using feedback as a stepping stone to success is to reframe our mindset about criticism. Instead of seeing criticism as a personal attack, we should view it as an opportunity for growth. Feedback provides us with valuable insights that can help us improve our skills and achieve our goals. By accepting criticism as a necessary part of the learning process, we can transform it into a positive experience that can propel us towards success.

Once we have adopted a growth mindset towards feedback, we can start to use it as a tool for self-improvement. The key to using feedback effectively is to listen actively and objectively. We should avoid becoming defensive or emotional and instead, focus on understanding the feedback. This involves asking clarifying questions and reflecting on the feedback to identify areas where we can improve.

After we have received feedback, we should use it to set goals and develop a plan for improvement. We should be specific about the changes we want to make and create actionable steps that will help us achieve our goals. It is also important to track our progress and celebrate our successes along the way. By using feedback to set goals and make progress, we can turn criticism into a stepping stone towards success.

Another way to use feedback as a stepping stone to success is to seek out feedback proactively. Instead of waiting for feedback to come to us, we should actively seek it out from our peers, mentors, and supervisors. This demonstrates a willingness to learn and improve, and can also provide us with valuable insights that we may not have considered before.

In addition to seeking out feedback, we should also give feedback to others. By providing constructive criticism to our colleagues and peers, we can help them improve their skills and achieve their goals.

CHAPTER SEVENTEEN

The Importance of Self-Reflection: Learning from Success and Failure Alike

Self-reflection is a powerful tool that can help individuals learn from both their successes and their failures. It allows us to take a step back, evaluate our experiences, and gain insights that can inform our future actions. Whether we have just achieved a major milestone or encountered a significant setback, self-reflection can help us make sense of our experiences and identify opportunities for growth and improvement.

When we succeed, it can be tempting to simply revel in our accomplishments and move on to the next challenge. However, taking the time to reflect on what we did right can help us understand why we were successful and how we can replicate that success in the future. For example, if we have just completed a challenging project, we might ask ourselves questions such as: What specific actions did I take that contributed to my success?

How did my strengths and skills play a role in achieving my goal?
What obstacles did I encounter, and how did I overcome them?
What could I have done differently to make the process smoother or more efficient?
How can I apply what I learned from this experience to future projects or endeavors?
By answering these questions, we can gain a deeper understanding of our strengths and weaknesses, as well as the specific strategies and behaviors that lead to success. This can help us approach future challenges with greater confidence and clarity, and avoid making the same mistakes twice.

On the other hand, when we experience failure or setbacks, self-reflection can help us identify the root causes of our difficulties and develop strategies for overcoming them. When we encounter failure, it is natural to feel disappointed, frustrated, or discouraged. However, rather than wallowing in these negative emotions, self-reflection can help us gain a more objective understanding of what went wrong and why. For example, if we have just received negative feedback from a supervisor, we might ask ourselves:

What specific behaviors or actions led to this feedback?
How did my own assumptions or biases contribute to the situation?
What could I have done differently to improve the outcome?
How can I learn from this experience to avoid similar mistakes in the future?
By approaching failure with a curious and open mindset, we can turn it into an opportunity for growth and

improvement. Rather than viewing failure as a reflection of our own worth or abilities, we can see it as a chance to learn and develop new skills.In both cases, self-reflection is most effective when approached with a sense of curiosity, openness, and non-judgment. Rather than simply evaluating our experiences in terms of success or failure, we can use self-reflection as a tool for deepening our self-awareness, gaining new insights, and developing a more nuanced understanding of ourselves and the world around us. By learning from both our successes and our failures, we can approach future challenges with greater clarity, confidence, and resilience.

CHAPTER EIGHTEEN

Overcome from ups and downs in relationship

The success of a love life can depend on many factors, including communication, trust, compatibility, mutual respect, and shared values. It's important for both partners to be willing to put in effort to make the relationship work and to be committed to each other.

It's also important to remember that no relationship is perfect, and there will be challenges and obstacles to overcome. It's how the couple navigates these challenges that can determine the success of their relationship.

Ultimately, the success of a love life is subjective and can vary from person to person. Some may define success as a long-lasting relationship that leads to marriage and a family, while others may define it as a fulfilling and happy partnership regardless of marital status.

SUCCESS OF LOVE LIFE-

The success of a love life is not entirely dependent on hard work. While effort and dedication are important in any relationship, there are many other factors that contribute to a healthy and fulfilling love life.

Some of these factors include:

Compatibility: A successful love life often begins with two people who are compatible with each other. Compatibility can include shared values, interests, and goals.

Communication: Good communication is key to building a strong and lasting relationship. Couples who communicate openly and honestly with each other are more likely to resolve conflicts and build a deeper connection.

Trust: Trust is essential in any relationship. Couples who trust each other are more likely to feel secure and confident in their love life.

Commitment: A successful love life requires commitment from both partners. Couples who are committed to each other are more likely to work through difficult times and stay together through thick and thin.

Emotional intelligence: Emotional intelligence is the ability to understand and manage your own emotions, as well as the emotions of others. Couples who possess emotional intelligence are better able to communicate effectively, resolve conflicts, and build a strong and lasting relationship.

While hard work can certainly play a role in the success of a love life, it is important to remember that it is not the only factor. A successful love life requires a combination of effort, compatibility, communication, trust, commitment, and emotional intelligence.

AGAIN,

Ups and downs are a natural part of any relationship, and they can be caused by a variety of factors such as differences in personality, communication issues, conflicting goals, and external stressors. It's important to remember that experiencing challenges in a relationship is not a sign of failure, but rather an opportunity for growth and improvement.

Here are some ways to navigate the ups and downs in a relationship:

Communication: Communication is key in any relationship. Be honest and open about your feelings, concerns, and expectations. Encourage your partner to do the same, and actively listen to each other.

Compromise: Relationships require compromise. Be willing to meet your partner halfway and find solutions that work for both of you.

Respect: Respect is crucial in a healthy relationship. Treat your partner with kindness, understanding, and empathy, even during difficult times.

Seek support: Don't be afraid to seek support from friends, family, or a therapist. Sometimes, an outside perspective can be helpful in resolving conflicts and improving the relationship.

Remember that every relationship is unique, and there is no one-size-fits-all approach to dealing with ups and downs. What's important is that you and your partner work together to find solutions that work for both of you, and that you remain committed to each other through the challenges.

9 798890 025289

Printed by Libri Plureos GmbH in Hamburg,
Germany